STEAM'S LAMENT

Bulleid's Merchant Navy, Q1, Leader & Other Works

Kevin Derrick

Strathwood

STEAM'S LAMENT

Bulleid's Merchant Navy, Q1, Leader & Other Works

© Strathwood Publishing 2021
ISBN 978-1-913390-25-9

Strathwood
4 Shuttleworth Road,
Elm Farm Industrial Estate,
Bedford, MK41 0EP
Telephone 01234 328792
Printed by Akcent Media, Ltd.

Certainly, Cost a Packet

In her final un-rebuilt condition 35001 Channel Packet storms away from Folkestone Central on 26 March 1959 with steam to spare for the road ahead. Just two months later, on 27 May she was taken into Eastleigh Works for her rebuild, emerging to traffic once more on 8 August 1959. The locomotive would also see a re-allocation recorded whilst still in works on 14 June from Stewarts Lane to the Western Section based out of Nine Elms.
Dr Terry Gough/The Transport Library

A chance to play spot the differences with these two shots, the first to the left is from March 1941 at Eastleigh against Channel Packet's post-war look from early 1946. In between times the locomotive had also seen service in a wartime black livery. *Strathwood Library Collection*

Until 1950 the Merchant Navy Pacifics were usually double manned with regular crews, although footplate cleanliness was always maintained the same could not always be said for their external appearance as here at Exmouth Junction in June 1949, in what were still very much austerity conditions. In this view we can again compare her with the previous views, among some of the most visible further modifications included new smoke deflectors. *Colour Rail*

Renumbering as 35001 along with a well-deserved repaint into the then new style of British Railway's blue livery with straw coloured numbering and lining completed with the large version of the early crest first took place in the autumn of 1949. This undated photograph shows her at Bournemouth soon afterwards. In December, the following year although her cab was modified at Eastleigh Works, she retained this blue livery, not going green until May 1952. Of note are the blackout shutters let into the tender sides, these would disappear on 35001 when its tender was modified and cut down in June 1956. *Colour Rail*

The air-smoothed curves of 35001 Channel Packet caught the attention of our cameraman visiting the engine shed at Exmouth Junction on 24 August 1954. Beneath those graceful lines was that ferocious 280psi boiler coupled to a coal hungry steel firebox. The boilers on these Pacifics were electrically welded and coupled to Nicholson thermic syphons supplying ample power to Bulleid's unique chain-driven valve gear through the outside-admission piston steam valves. In turn this power was laid down to the track via those distinctive Bulleid-Firth-Brown driving wheels.

R.C. Riley/The Transport Treasury

Going well and climbing from Tonbridge up Hildenborough bank 35001 Channel Packet has full command of a heavy up boat train. She ran with this modified tender after June 1956 until rebuilt in the summer of 1959. *Rail Photoprints*

One of the modifications made as part of the rebuilding process was a redesign of the ashpan as a self-emptying type with a rocker grate above it. In this view at Eastleigh on 2 March 1963 we can also see the new 5,250-gallon replacement tender tank fitted the previous month during a light intermediate overhaul in the works. *Peter Simmonds*

In this earlier view taken at Exmouth Junction on 31 August 1959, just three weeks after 35001's release from rebuilding we can see that the background to the nameplates were then painted black rather than red in the previous scene. Withdrawal would come on 22 November 1964, although perhaps historically significant albeit much rebuilt of course, 35001 went for scrapping to Bird's of Morriston five months later. *The Bluebell Museum Archive*

A mid-fifties view of 35002 Union Castle finds this 72A Exmouth Junction allocated example heading west with the returning milk empties through Wimbledon. *Rail Photoprints*

For a short while in 1952 35002 Union Castle ran paired with a blue tender although the locomotive itself had already been repainted in lined green livery during the early summer of 1951. On 17 May 1953 she is back in just the one livery once more sitting in the bay platform at Southampton Central with a service for Salisbury and most likely Exeter Central too. The original forward rake of the cab design and the profiled tender to match Bulleid's coach designs show up well against the lines of the rebuilt versions in these two views, firstly at Eastleigh around 1952 and Nine Elms just before she was withdrawn in February 1964. *Photos: Rail Photoprints & Strathwood Library Collection*

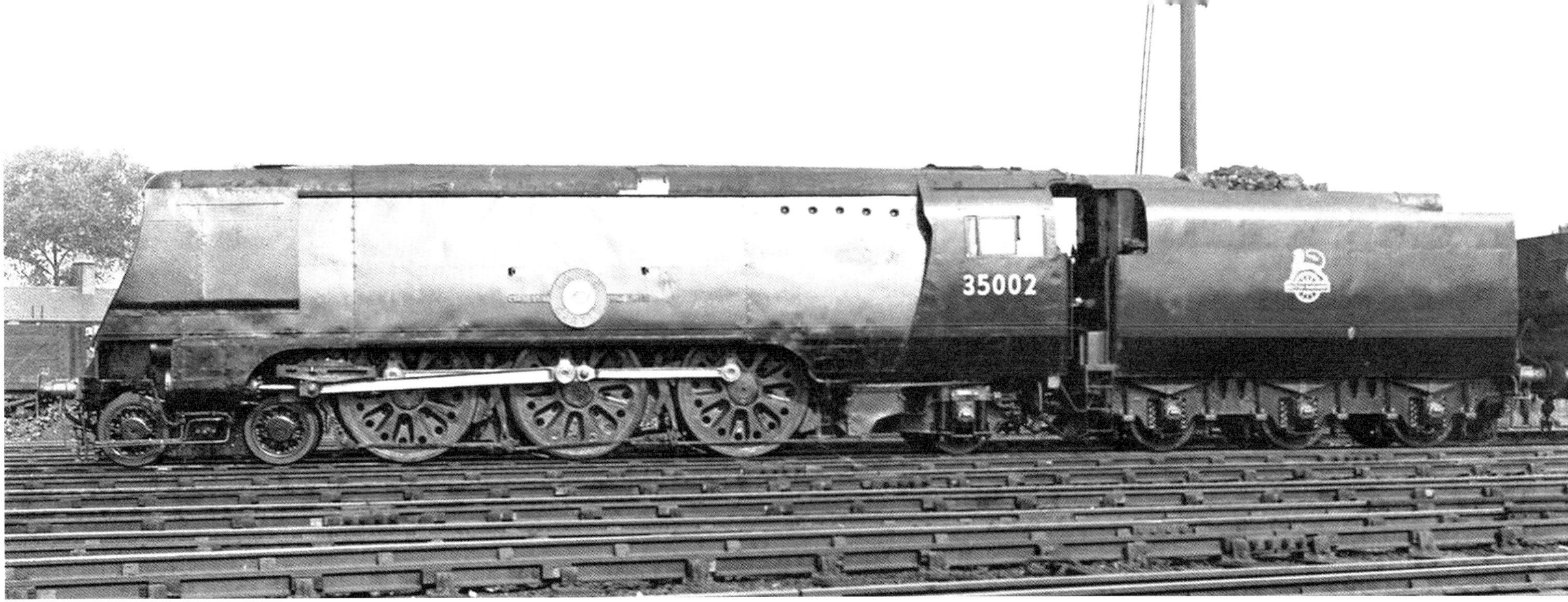
35002

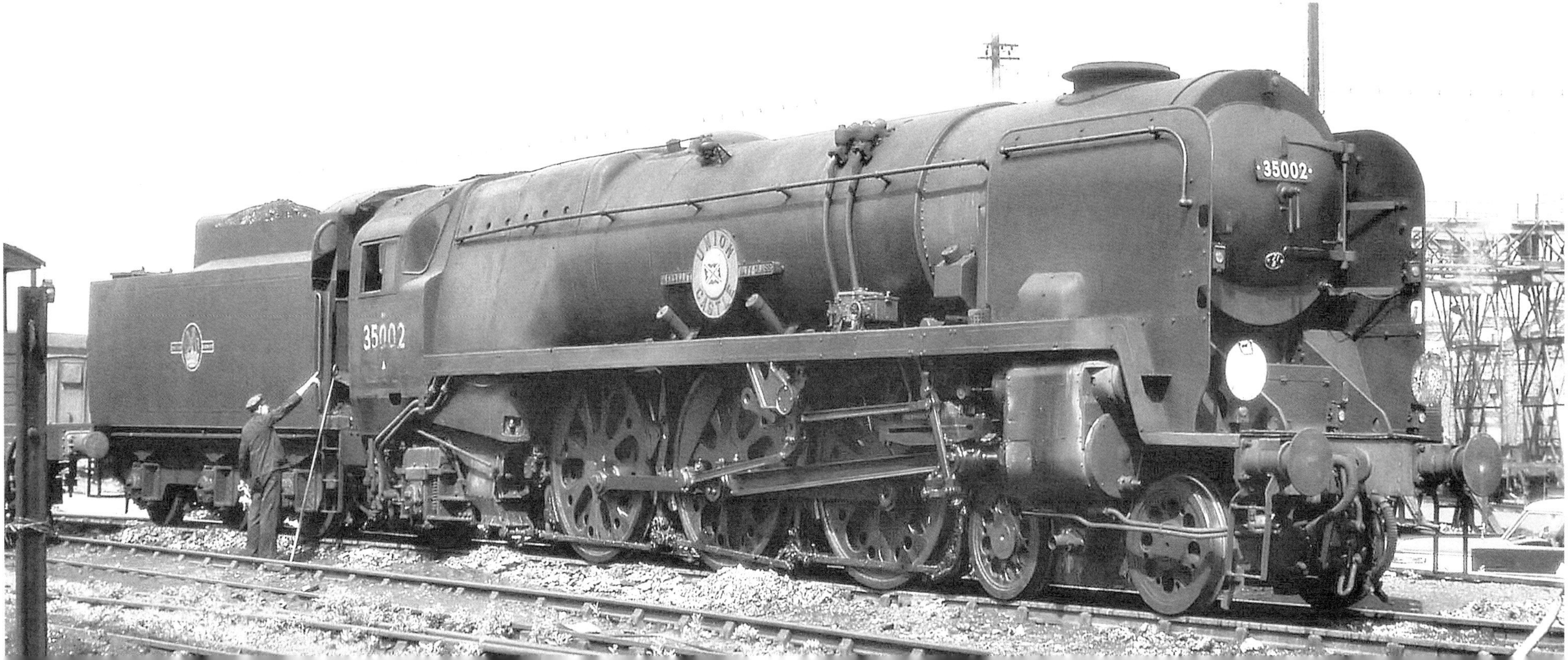
35002
UNION CASTLE
35002

Standards were slipping by the start of the sixties as we see the now rebuilt 35002 Union Castle letting her public appearance down against the well-presented Pullman stock of today's Bournemouth Belle as they run through Pokesdown on the down fast line. *Rail Archive Stephenson*

Opposite: With a modified cab and in the attractive lined blue livery 35003 Royal Mail speeds through Brookwood on 28 July 1951. The support joint for the limpet board boiler casing is now very noticeable on these next seven of the class to be released to traffic, until their rebuilding changed their appearance completely. *Colour Rail*

Originally to save both some weight and valuable steel sheeting which was in short supply, Oliver Bulleid specified asbestos-fibreboard side cladding with a horizontal rib for strengthening along the boiler sides for numbers 21C3 – 21C10. The first built locomotive from this second batch now renumbered as 35003 Royal Mail speeds west through Surbiton with what appears to be one of Bulleid's tavern cars eight vehicles back along this twelve-coach train around 1950. After her rebuilding in August 1959, 35003 Royal Mail shuffles about light engine to take on a departure from Waterloo under the gaze of the busy top-grade signalmen controlling the station throat around 1962. *Rail Photoprints & Rail Online*

Opposite: Another undated shot of 35003 Royal Mail this time from around 1964 finds her on the centre roads at Bournemouth Central. Withdrawn in July 1967, she would cover 1,131,793 miles in traffic, but only 272,009 of these would be in this rebuilt condition, so one wonders about the economics of the exercise. Some of the Nine Elms' men thought well of 35003 to be the fastest of the class. **www.Anistr.com**

Below: Standing alongside the carriage servicing sheds at Exeter in July 1957, 35004 Cunard White Star shows no signs of her previous brush with a German aircraft during November 1942 near Whimple. Her locomotive crew that day were not injured but certainly had a story to tell their colleagues, the locomotive was soon repaired and back once again in regular service. *Rail Photoprints*

On 16 May 1964, 35004 Cunard White Star was in charge of the 13.00 Waterloo to Exeter emerging from Buckhorn Weston tunnel. She had been allocated alternately between Exmouth Junction and Salisbury throughout her career, however this would soon change after 14 September 1964 with a move to Bournemouth shed. As fate would decree, she went into a bout of uncontrollable slipping near Hook one day in October 1965. She was assessed for possible repairs but deemed beyond economic hope and dumped at Eastleigh as a cripple unfit to travel to a scrapyard, she was dealt with by the flying cutters of Messrs George Cohen's on-site during February 1966.
Strathwood Library Collection

Opposite: Taken into Eastleigh Works just days after Nationalisation in January 1948, 35005 Canadian Pacific would be sent out into service once more on 20 March fitted with a mechanical stoker still numbered as s21C5, then as here when seen at Pirbright now as 35005 in malachite green lined in yellow with sunshine lettering, clearly demonstrating its ability to lay an effective smoke screen in its wake. *Rail Photoprints*

In early 1950, 35005 Canadian Pacific was repainted into blue livery having also gained a modified wedge-shaped cab. The locomotive was sent to Rugby where we see her being prepared for entry to the testing station in February 1950. Once completed the stoker was removed for further comparative testing with hand firing of the locomotive during that April. The mechanical stoker was then refitted for a further year back in service. The use of the Berkley stoker caused many issues with the locomotive leaving trails of black smoke and coal dust in its wake, making it unpopular in many circles including dining car staff and Pullman stewards as the fine coal dust penetrated the coach interiors and soiled both the fresh white table linen and their uniforms, not to mention passenger's food and drinks. In between time on 22 September 1950, 35005 had massively failed near Woking requiring a complete new right-hand cylinder and rods before returning to traffic on 17 November 1950. We next find her balanced on the Nine Elms turntable on 15 June 1957, having been painted into the now standard British Railway's lined green livery since early 1954. **Both: Rail Archive Stephenson**

Demonstrating the effectiveness of the smoke deflectors after their rebuilding 35005 Canadian Pacific speeds an up express towards New Milton during the harsh winter of 1962-63. She would be a regular through here after her rebuilding at Eastleigh Works in May 1959, with subsequent allocations to Bournemouth and Weymouth. We next see her coming off the stock of the Home Counties Railway Society's Somerset & Dorset rail tour at Bournemouth on 7 June 1964, having just made the 108-mile run from Waterloo in good time. The record would show that she did not make the magic one million miles in service, but instead a creditable 976,806 with 344,484 being completed in this rebuilt guise. Upon withdrawal on 10 October 1965 a period of storage ensued alongside the shed at Feltham, until a move to Weymouth was made in January 1966. The next movement turned out to be beneficial as it was to Woodham's scrapyard in Barry. Sanctuary within the preservation movement came first via Steamtown in Carnforth in 1973. Thankfully, she is still with us today, long gone is her footplatemen's nickname of "Canadian Pathetic" from her early days with the mechanical stoker.
Photos: www.Anistr.com & Tony Butcher

A most delightfully Southern Nouveau scene alongside the ferro-concrete structure of Exmouth Junction engine shed in 1950 with 35006 Peninsular & Oriental S.N. Co. still wearing her malachite green livery. Inspired by his earlier work with Gresley on the 2-8-2 Class P2 locomotives for the LNER, Bulleid cast thoughts towards not only a 2-8-2 for the Southern Railway but also a 4-8-2. Turntable limitations together with uproar from the Civil Engineer soon stunted these ambitions, although approval was given for two 2-8-2s to be built. Concerns over possible final acceptance of these led to the design becoming what we see at his Merchant Navy Pacifics instead. *www.Anistr.com*

Although the welded steel boilers for the class would be one of their most redeeming features, they would be both heavy and expensive. At the time when the first ten of the Merchant Navy Class were being built in 1941, the Second World War was not going very well and the skills to electrically weld such items were scarce. As a result, the work was put out to the North British Locomotive Company in Glasgow. On 2 June 1951, 35006 Peninsular & Oriental S.N. Co. was approaching Basingstoke with a down train already fitted with the third of what would be five boilers during its working life of less than twenty-three years!
Rail Archive Stephenson

Having now just received her fourth boiler she is seen fresh from the works here at Eastleigh on 5 September 1953, having just been repainted into British Railway's green livery.
Strathwood Library Collection

One of the ten Merchant Navy Pacifics to be rebuilt at Eastleigh during 1959 was Salisbury's 35006 Peninsular & Oriental S.N. Co. Here she is standing in the shed yard at Eastleigh on 18 July 1962. Throughout her working life she would remain a Salisbury engine, being withdrawn in August 1964 and then dumped here at Eastleigh until once again being fortunately sent to Woodham's yard rather than the other busy scrap dealers of the day in March 1965. Rescue would come in March 1983 for preservation although to do so required a completely new tender. *The Transport Treasury*

Opposite: Salisbury's 35007 Aberdeen Commonwealth blows off furiously with her tender well filled for a run back eastwards from Exeter Central around 1955. This was the year when during a general overhaul at Eastleigh her safety valves were also repositioned further back towards the cab and firebox along with a reduction of her boiler pressure from a fearsome 280psi to 250psi. This modification which would be applied to all the class, thus reduced a problem that was liable to occur as the locomotives came to a halt sometimes abruptly allowing boiling water to be ejected rather than excess steam. *Rail Online*

An early morning Salisbury to Waterloo service obeys the speed restrictions through Clapham Junction behind 35007 Aberdeen Commonwealth now coupled to her rebuilt 5,250-gallon tender which she carried from September 1956 until September 1966. At this point she was paired up with the modified 6,000-gallon tender from the now withdrawn 35016 Elders Fyffes which is she next carrying here departing Southampton Central early in 1967. She ran until the last month of Southern steam in July 1967, achieving 1,318,765 miles the highest for the class, with 519,466 as a rebuilt locomotive after May 1958. *Photos: Rail Archive Stephenson & Strathwood Library Collection*

There are a few meaty looking lumps of coal in the tender of 35008 Orient Line when seen on shed at Nine Elms on 24 September 1955. The locomotive had been sent new into traffic in June 1942 in a wartime black livery. On 10 June 1947 she suffered a collision damaging her front end with some electric stock at Waterloo. Eastleigh's repairs at the time fitted her with the later style of wedge cab and new boiler and firebox along with the improved smoke deflectors, topped off with a fresh malachite green livery. The repaint into British Railway's lined green being made in May 1952. In rebuilt condition from May 1957, she remained in service until July 1967, here she looks to be in fine fettle heading for the Dorset coast with the Bournemouth Belle in 1962 passing through Weybridge. *Rail Archive Stephenson & Strathwood Library Collection*

Opposite: Today's Top Link driver has taken a step back to visually check everything as part of his diligent preparations before his departure from Waterloo behind 35008 Orient Line during June 1964. Part of the AWS (Audible Warning System) equipment fitted to this locomotive during the early months of 1960 can be seen above the front bufferbeam. *Strathwood Library Collection*

There would be no such security of AWS for the footplate crews of 35009 Shaw Savill for another ten years when this view was taken during 1950 passing Durnsford Road Power Station at Wimbledon with a down express. To the left we can see the unique electric shunter - DS74 - which operated at the power station, it was built at Nine Elms works in 1899 for use on the Waterloo and City Line being transferred to Durnsford Road in 1915. *Rail Photoprints*

A busy scene at Waterloo around 1962 as one young lad witnesses the departure of 35009 Shaw Savill following a Portsmouth bound rake of 4-CORs up the bank towards Vauxhall. *Chris Wilson Collection*

An earlier view soon after 35009 Shaw Savill was rebuilt in March 1957, finds her blowing off ready to head for Waterloo with the up Atlantic Coast Express, interestingly with an ex-LNER Gresley coach tucked in behind the tender as they wait in the centre road for their own departure. *Rail Online*

Three early livery variations for 35010 Blue Star, firstly in malachite green soon after Nationalisation at Salisbury. Then ready to depart from Waterloo during its short period in blue from November 1949 until November 1951, finally in British Railway's lined green with the down Devon Belle passing through Farnborough on 11 September 1954.

Photos: Strathwood Library Collection & Colour Rail

During November 1956, 35010 Blue Star was set aside and stored at Bournemouth shed pending entry to Eastleigh for rebuilding. She would be the first from the initial batch of ten locomotives so far to be sent for a rebuild, as the opening rebuilds had all been from the twenty later built locomotives. One of the aspects of 35010's rebuild would be the need to replace the mainframes ahead of her cylinders. We see her firstly still carrying her earlier style of British Railway's crest as late as 8 July 1961 in this broadside view at Nine Elms. Her next visit to Eastleigh Works during October and November would see her sent back into service with the later emblem in place. *Colour Rail*

In this earlier view we see her in full flight approaching Surbiton on 22 March 1957, just over two months after her rebuild on today's Royal Wessex service. *Tony Butcher*

The flared cast iron chimney of the rebuilds shows up well in this view, it was much heavier than the original Bulleid stovepipe design, placed directly above the Lemaitre blast pipe within the smokebox. This is an easy filling-in turn for 35010 Blue Star accelerating effortlessly away from Wilton (South) with an all-stations stopper on 30 July 1961. *Hugh Ballantyne/Rail Photoprints*

The up Bournemouth Belle approaches Micheldever during 1950 with 35011 General Steam Navigation from Nine Elms in charge. The fireman's duties were eased once they had mastered the use of the treadle-operated steam-powered firebox doors, along with electric lighting. Although wise firemen would still carry oil lamps and trim them correctly just in case. This second batch of ten engines originally numbered 21C11 – 21C20 were delivered between December 1944 and June 1945. In anticipation of peacetime, they were constructed with numerous detail differences to the first ten locomotives. Among these were changes to the designs of the smoke deflectors, front side valances, also the contours of the cab and the tender along with a further 100-gallons of water capacity available. *Rail Archive Stephenson*

Although the modification process for the Merchant Navy's tenders commenced in 1952 with the removal of the raves to allow footplate crews easier access for watering, we can see 35011 General Steam Navigation was to still be dealt with when seen ready to head away from Bournemouth Central on 4 May 1957. A visit to Eastleigh for a light intermediate overhaul six weeks later would see her turn arrive. Our second view a few months later shows her changed appearance with a modified tender along with the newer emblem affixed and changes to how the cab was lined out too when seen at Exmouth Junction. *Photos: Rail Archive Stephenson & Rail Photoprints*

With what is believed to be the down Bournemouth Belle just to the north of Bournemouth West, 35011 General Steam Navigation is seen in the mid-sixties running without it's 71B Bournemouth shed plate. We see her next as a regular on this route until February 1966 passing Tunnel Junction at Southampton. She lost her middle crank axle early in 1966 probably as a spare to keep one of her sisters in traffic and then as a result went into store at Eastleigh before being towed to Woodham's yard in Barry. It seems this move was carried out with the locomotive appearing as almost an Atlantic. No doubt the connecting rods and motion were piled into the tender and the boiler emptied of water before travelling, otherwise she might have fallen foul of the civil engineering department for her axle loading. Because of her woebegone state at Barry, she was overlooked for preservation until March 1989, thus she spent twenty-two years in active service, followed by twenty-two further years at Barry and has been within the preservation movement now for over thirty-four years as dedicated enthusiasts bravely work on restoring 35011 General Steam Navigation back to her original condition as built.

Both: Rail Archive Stephenson

With a healthy load of at least twelve coaches in tow 35012 United States Lines crosses the River Avon near Christchurch after her tender was rebuilt during her first general overhaul at Eastleigh Works in the summer of 1952. With an allocation history revolving around Nine Elms, Bournemouth and Weymouth sheds during her twenty-two-year working career it can be easily assumed she spent most of her time on this route rather than the runs to Exeter and Salisbury. Being one of the earlier rebuilds to be completed in February 1957 she retained the small early style of crest just as the later design was about to become standard. Indeed, here she is a few months later that year on the ash road at Nine Elms on 15 June as a young-looking fireman keeps a wary eye upon our cameraman. The nickname of Spam Cans was quickly bestowed upon the class when they were new during a war-torn London in 1941. However, as the Light Pacifics appeared they took over the name with the Merchant Navy Pacifics being referred to as "Channel Packets" after the first of the class or simply as "Packets". Some Cockney London men then derived this it seems into "Flannel Jackets". Inevitably perhaps some footplate men preferred the locomotives in their original form over the rebuilds and vice versa of course, always a subject for debate for those who knew them.
Both: Rail Archive Stephenson

To prove that 35012 United States Lines did some work on the Salisbury and Exeter lines of course we see her striking away from the speed restrictions at Clapham Junction with the down Atlantic Coast Express during her second of three spells allocated to 70A Nine Elms. On 24 April 1964, 35012 United States Lines was appropriately freshened up and chosen to haul the now preserved and cosmetically overhauled Gresley Class A4, 60008 Dwight D. Eisenhower to Southampton Docks. The A4 was to be loaded and shipped to the American Railroad Museum at Green Bay. In fine condition herself 35012 had also hauled the dignitaries down from Waterloo. It appears the museum's president was taken by 35012 United States Lines and suggested they would like it too for their collection upon withdrawal. Unfortunately, all this goodwill and opportunity came to nought. For when withdrawal came in April 1967, 35012 was put into storage firstly at Nine Elms and then again at Weymouth until 23 March 1968. At which point she was hauled to Cashmore's scrapyard at Newport where we see her awaiting a grizzly fate soon afterwards in the company of 34044 Woolacombe, as the cutters eagerly made their way through scrapping the last remnants of the Southern's steam fleet.

Photos: Rail Archive Stephenson & Strathwood Library Collection

The fireman aboard 21C13 Blue Funnel has ensured he will not run short of coal by the look of that fully loaded tender perhaps only just within loading gauge as they sweep into Clapham Junction during 1948 en-route to Bournemouth. Even through extensive trackwork such as here the fine Bulleid three-point suspension fitted to the trailing truck would give a much smoother ride than most other classes. *Rail Photoprints*

Opposite: This time on Devon Belle duty, 35013 Blue Funnel heads west from Winchfield on 2 September 1949 now sporting its new number but as yet no British Railways tender lettering. The use of these dramatic winged promotional headboards necessitated the hanging ridge on the smoke deflectors on both the original Merchant Navy and Light Pacifics. *Rail Archive Stephenson*

During 1949, 35013 Blue Funnel which had recently been repainted once again in malachite green complete with broad yellow lining along with British Railways in the originally favoured style of Gill Sans numerals and lettering works the heavy load of fourteen coaches of today's ACE up the bank out of Waterloo through Vauxhall. Although at this time the headboards for both the Atlantic Coast Express as it was officially known, and The Devon Belle were similar in style only the latter was blessed with the winged side boards as well. *Rail Archive Stephenson*

When new in 1945 she originally wore the nameplates as Blue Funnel Line for a brief time only, she was generally known as simply Blue Funnel. The nameplates were cast in three pieces with additional enamel centre plates displaying the appropriate emblems for the shipping line, the nameplates being fitted so that the flags would always appear to be flowing correctly in the wind with the locomotive in forward travel. *Colour Rail*

The third of the class to be treated to a full rebuild including a new boiler would be 35013 Blue Funnel released back into service in May 1956. Just before this she was positioned by the Eastleigh Works office block which affords us this splendid, elevated view with her rods set just so with her tender still empty. Another new boiler would be fitted to her during her next general overhaul at Eastleigh during March through to May 1961. *Colour Rail*

Opposite: We next see her making the stop at Salisbury during April 1964 working an up Atlantic Coast Express, she was being watered and having her coal dragged forward as the footplate crews changed over. Although she had been allocated to 72A Exmouth Junction she was officially allocated as Western Region stock from 1 January that year as her former shed changed regions. On 14 September she would be placed in the care of 71B Bournemouth for the next twenty-five months. *Rail Photoprints*

Left: No doubt a treasured moment for this young lad as his father perhaps, explains some of the workings within the cab of the footplate crew of 35013 Blue Funnel upon arrival at Waterloo in July 1965. *Rail Photoprints*

The smokebox door bares evidence of some recent hard running and ash accumulation as 35013 Blue Funnel heads for Bournemouth and Weymouth one sunny summer's day around the same period. *Rail Archive Stephenson*

This photograph must have been taken around May 1949 as 35014 Nederland Line has just been released from Eastleigh Works with a modified cab and renumbered from 21C14. In this condition and livery, it brings the best out the very stylish lines on a Merchant Navy Pacific in your author's opinion. Upon rebuilding those distinctive nameplates required a curved infill piece to be manufactured to allow them to be fixed to the new rounded boiler casings.

Photos: Strathwood Library Collection

We can see in this shot taken near Brockenhurst soon after her rebuild in the summer of 1956, 35014 Nederland Line would be another example released to traffic with the earlier small emblem on her tender. *Rail Archive Stephenson*

Salisbury was a great location for spotters on the platforms into the early 1960s, in these two scenes from 3 July 1962 we see it is all hands on deck for the swift turnaround of the locomotive crews and the refreshing of the catering facilities. Nine Elms allocated 35014 Nederland Line draws in with the down ACE. In earlier days locomotives were exchanged here but after 1950 with a greater availability of Bulleids, they just exchanged footplate crews. The London based men help their Exmouth Junction based colleagues to quickly get their Merchant Navy ready to head for Exeter where this Pacific will finally come off. *Both: Bluebell Museum Archive*

When compiling photographs of any class of steam engines it becomes clear that some locomotives appear frequently while others are very much camera shy. This most likely was reflected by the notes of spotters from the day too. Sometimes it can be attributed to certain locomotives being regular on overnight turns, meaning they only ever appear in print on shed or in works. While others such as 35014 Nederland Line managed to get themselves very well photographed indeed. The exception seems to be during the locomotive's short twelve-month allocation to Stewarts Lane across 1955 – 1956. Another reason for her frequency certainly once rebuilt could be down to her higher mileage in this form at 545,583 miles coupled with an increased number of photographers, certainly after 1960. Here we see her first departing Salisbury past Tunnel Junction, then attracting a group of admiring spotters all no doubt eager for a possible invite up onto the footplate before departure time from Waterloo.
Photos: Rail Archive Stephenson & Strathwood Library Collection

The changing face and liveries of the Bournemouth Belle as the Southern Railway's influence morphed into the early days of British Railways can be compared here. Firstly as 35015 Rotterdam Lloyd which has just received her new modified cab and renumbered from 21C15 remains in Bulleid's preferred malachite green livery complete with sunshine lining as she confidently passes Nine Elms on 4 July 1949. Almost two years later we catch the same locomotive once again on this prestige duty approaching Basingstoke on 2 June 1951. She is now resplendent in British Railway's blue livery complete with the proud new nationalised railway's emblem upon her tender. Also note the subtle livery changes on the leading Pullman brakes between both photographs. *Photos: Rail Archive Stephenson & The Transport Treasury*

Opposite: A one time regular on the Golden Arrow boat train on the Eastern Section was 35015 Rotterdam Lloyd in both original guise and later in her rebuilt form after June 1958, while she was based out of Stewarts Lane from June 1956 until June 1959. Here we see her passing Willesborough just to the east of Ashford which if the date recorded is correct of 6 June 1959, just before her transfer to Nine Elms. *Colour Rail*

A return to glory and Pullman duties once again this time on the Western Section as she backs onto the stock for the Bournemouth Belle at Waterloo on 4 March 1961. Her demise would come just a few years later in February 1964 upon withdrawal she would head north to the yard of The Slag Reduction Company in Rotherham for breaking up. *Colour Rail*

Left: This undated shot of 35016 Elders Fyffes passing the somewhat crowded EMU depot at Durnsford Road in Wimbledon was most likely taken on a Sunday somewhere between May 1950 and February 1953 when the locomotive was in service wearing British Railway's lined blue livery. *Rail Photoprints*

Right: The light intermediate overhaul at Eastleigh Works during February and March 1953 then saw 35016 Elders Fyffes turned out in the new officially decreed lined green livery. As a long term Nine Elms based locomotive from 1945 until 1964, she would have been a commonplace sight charging through London's suburbs such as here at Surbiton once again working another West of England express. *www.Anistr.com*

Once more captured in suburbia 35016 Elders Fyffes will take a different route today as she passes Clapham with an afternoon train for Bournemouth on 2 March 1957. Eleven days later she would enter Eastleigh Works for her rebuild, having completed 467,181 miles since she was new twelve years earlier. Back in traffic as a rebuild after 17 April 1957, she would go on to deliver another 433,456 miles in service. We catch her awaiting departure from Bournemouth West looking well-groomed to head the up Bournemouth Belle during 1959. The following year she would be fitted with AWS and a speedometer, at last the footplate crews could judge their speeds and signalling with some assistance.
Photos: R.C. Riley/The Transport Treasury & Rail Archive Stephenson

Two fellow enthusiasts admire 35016 Elders Fyffes during her Basingstoke stop heading for the Dorset coast on 17 July 1964. The locomotive's long association with Nine Elms shed would come to an end after 14 September that year with a reallocation to Weymouth, although of course she would still be a regular visitor at her former London residence. But not for too long though, as she was withdrawn on 8 August the following year and dumped at Weymouth until November. On the 13th of the month, she was noted heading to South Wales being hauled dead, her destination being Bird's of Risca for scrapping. *Rail Archive Stephenson*

The word was out among the young spotters of Leeds, here at Copley Hill that they could cop 35017 Belgian Marine being serviced at the shed nearby between 25 and 28 May 1948 during the Locomotive Exchanges.
Strathwood Library Collection

As we see her setting off from Kings Cross during her four days on this route it was later reported by a reliable source that she climbed Holloway Bank fast faster than any LNER Pacifics with a comparable load.
Strathwood Library Collection

Complete with a Stanier 4,000-gallon tender most importantly allowing her to pick up water from the troughs en-route, 35017 Belgian Marine passes Wood Green in late May 1948 in charge of the 13.10 Kings Cross to Leeds, with the fireman putting a few rounds into the firebox.
Rail Archive Stephenson

Resplendent now in its recently applied lined blue livery 35017 Belgian Marine stands on home ground at Nine Elms in the latter half of 1949. Aside from her exploits for a few days on the route to Leeds, 35017 was also put to work between Euston and Carlisle which certainly confirmed the locomotive's desire for coal. *Rail Photoprints*

The next repaint came for 35017 Belgian Marine in March 1953 during a light intermediate repair took her back into green, but in the approved British Railway's lined style with an as yet un-modified tender as seen here between Bournemouth Central and journey's end for the Bournemouth Belle at the Dorset resort's West station soon afterwards. Her next general overhaul took place in the summer of 1954, followed three years later with a full rebuild completed on 30 March 1957. The following week she caught our cameraman's attention in her new guise with steam to spare at an almost deserted Waterloo station on Sunday 7 April. *Photos: Rail Archive Stephenson & Colour Rail*

Running under clear signals 35017 Belgian Marine is going full steam ahead through Earlsfield with an Exeter service on All Fools Day in 1958. AWS equipment would be fitted in the autumn of the following year, the addition of a speedometer came exactly three years to the day after the photograph opposite was recorded. In the scene above taken at Nine Elms during 1962 we can see the long overdue speedometer affixed to the trailing driving wheel. Transferred to Weymouth in September 1964, 35017 Belgian Marine worked her last duty from here being withdrawn officially on 17 July 1966. She then went into storage at Eastleigh briefly before being towed to Buttigieg's scrapyard in Newport on 25 September 1966.

Photos: *Tony Butcher & Strathwood Library Collection*

In this early 1948 view taken at Bournemouth West 21C18 British India Line will soon become 35018 with her new ownership. We can also see the problems possibly for the fireman getting the bag of the water crane into the tender filler over the side raves with these two differing height water cranes. During May, the same year the cab of 35018 was modified to accept a Flaman speed recorder as the locomotive was to provide part of the data required for the Locomotive Exchanges as she was rostered onto Waterloo – Exeter workings. In September 1949, 35018 emerged from overhaul in lined blue livery which was short-lived. She was soon repainted into lined green in early July 1951, in this guise we see her setting out from Waterloo shortly afterwards. The following year 35018 was matched up with the specially adapted coal weighing tender no.3343 for three months of tests before next acquiring tender no.3346 which had come from 35024 East Asiatic Company. After running 504,900 in service 35018 British India Line was sent to Eastleigh for a general overhaul which led to her becoming the first of the Merchant Navy Class to be rebuilt, returning to traffic on 14 February 1956.
Strathwood Library Collection & Rail Archive Stephenson

Upon being selected as the first of the class to be rebuilt, inevitably some lessons would be learned amidst this process for 35018 British India Line during her general overhaul/rebuild which begun on 6 November 1955. She would be released from Eastleigh for trials on 14 February 1956. The easiest way to spot her from the remainder of the rebuilt locomotives was from the left-hand side with the less aesthetic bends to the ejector piping around the nameplate. These two views of her on Bournemouth Belle duty show this well, firstly in 1957 approaching Surbiton, then secondly near Hinton Admiral the same year. Fortunately for the preservation movement she was purchased for scrap by Woodham's of Barry upon withdrawal in August 1964, just eight and a half years after being totally rebuilt, having covered 451,644 miles in this condition.

Photos: Tony Butcher
& Rail Archive Stephenson

Seen early in 1948 with Bournemouth's engine shed as a backdrop French Line C.G.T was still running as 21C19 complete with her original cab design which was modified during March and early April for the locomotive to take part in the Locomotive Exchanges. Making a rousing start from Paddington in May 1948 during these Locomotive Exchanges 35019 French Line C.G.T was rostered to work the 13.30 Paddington to Plymouth, with overnight servicing at Laira then return on the 08.30 Plymouth to Paddington. Although the locomotive suffered severe slipping on the steep gradients of South Devon, her capabilities still allowed for a full recovery of all lost time with her 500-ton load to arrive within the scheduled timings.
Mike Morant Collection & Rail Archive Stephenson

Once again paired up with that Stanier tender 35019 French Line C.G.T is next seen departing Kings Cross with the 13.10 regular service to Leeds in early May 1948. By the 28th of the month she was back at Eastleigh Works being refitted to her original tender with her exploits within the Locomotive Exchanges over. The same locomotive was chosen most appropriately to be dressed up and for her new British Railway's lined blue livery to be fully bulled up for the visit of the French President, Vincent Jules Auriol to head his Pullman car special from Dover to Victoria on 7 March 1950. This most impressive ensemble is seen soon after departure from Dover, the Pullman cars complete with white rooves except for the party's luggage van at the rear although repainted for the occasion almost lets the side down. A few months later 35019 French Line C.G.T was once again restored to this impressive condition but without the headboard to work a royal special from Waterloo to Sherborne and return.

Photos: Rail Archive Stephenson & Strathwood Library Collection

Opposite: In early 1952 Eastleigh Works fitted 35019 French Line C.G.T. with a single exhaust with a flared petticoat thus giving it a distinctive exhaust note akin it seems to a Drummond Class T14 Paddlebox in full cry. In this view of her basking in the sunshine outside Bournemouth's shed on 8 July 1953 the experiment unique to 35019 had another five months to go before it was replaced with a single blast pipe and a small diameter chimney. These tests cannot have been a success as 35019 was refitted with a multiple blastpipe thirteen months later. *Colour Rail*

An opportunity for a catch up on the gossip for the experienced men while their juniors break into a sweat attending to the coaling and watering needs of 35019 French Line C.G.T during their albeit brief crew changeover on this down West of England service during 1963 at Salisbury. *Strathwood Library Collection*

Opposite: Nine Elms allocated 35019 French Line C.G.T. appears to be very well kept perhaps after a recent special duty as it was almost seven months since her last light intermediate overhaul at Eastleigh, when she was seen at Weymouth on 3 October 1963. *Rail Photoprints*

The same cannot be said in these two views of her a couple of years later as she was seen at Waterloo on 24 June 1965, now carrying a 70G Weymouth shed code on her smokebox. Withdrawal was soon to arrive on 5 September, with storage at Nine Elms before heading to Cashmore's of Newport with stops along the way at Feltham and Gloucester.
Both: Strathwood Library Collection

Prepared as a reserve locomotive for the Locomotive Exchanges 35020 Bibby Line was not called upon, soon after she is seen just before departure from Waterloo somewhere between 8 May and 3 June while she was still paired to a Stanier tender. Her unique extended smoke deflectors also fitted for the exchanges however remained throughout subsequent repaints into both blue as here at Eastleigh during 1950, then into green in 1952 until finally rebuilt during early 1956. Note the sandbox filler sliding cover within the extensions, no wonder ladders and trestles were provided at engine sheds!

Photos: Strathwood Library Collection & Colour Rail

Destined to become the second of the class to benefit from rebuilding 35020 Bibby Line still had another four years of hard work to perform beforehand when seen emerging from Honiton tunnel at the head of a West of England express in 1952. *Rail Archive Stephenson*

After Nationalisation, the running costs and problems associated with the Merchant Navy Pacifics were already under the gaze of the British Railways Board with a desire to somehow effect economies and improve their performance. In March 1953 when 35020 Bibby Line complete with her already rebuilt tender was recorded departing from Southampton Central, the last straw was about to be drawn. Two months later 35020 Bibby Line came to grief at Crewkerne with a broken crank axle. As a result, the whole class were stopped for safety checks. Fourteen of the class were found to have similar flaws. Under the supervision of R.G. Jarvis, a major redesign was undertaken with 35018 British India Line being the first to be rebuilt in early 1956. Second of these rebuilds would be 35020 Bibby Line following in late April a few weeks later. Here we see her Nine Elms based driver oiling around in all the new places now requiring his attention once rebuilt before departure from Waterloo on 3 September the same year. Meanwhile a young family man peers into what appears to him perhaps to be a brand-new locomotive. By the end of 1959, all thirty of the class had been rebuilt.
Both: The Transport Treasury

Seen soon after being rebuilt in 1956, 35020 Bibby Line found itself paired back once again with a high-sided 6,000-gallon tender, suitably lined out rather than the intended modified one which was later fitted on 14 July 1956. In this configuration 35020 was thus able to conduct dynamometer car testing between Waterloo and Exeter from late May through into June 1956, as it was better to retain all the testing cables between the locomotive and the dynamometer car. The locomotive's hybrid appearance caught our photographer's eye in the lines that summer at Nine Elms. The pipe above the left-hand side nameplate in the lower study carries steam to the blower which would be used for drawing up the fire when the regulator was in the closed position and to reduce smoke when standing in stations.
Both: Strathwood Library Collection

On a cold and bright November morning during 1957, 35020 Bibby Line storms through Surbiton station on the down fast line with today's Atlantic Coast Express. Unlike some summer Saturdays there would be no call for a relief service to be run today. In early 1965, 35020 Bibby Line arrived at Eastleigh Works for assessment for repairs, the decision was not favourable, and as a result she was withdrawn on 14 February. Probably after being robbed for spares she was swiftly cut up in the works by the first week of March 1965. As an aside we wonder just how the distinctive Southern Railway concrete platform lamp came to be in this state? *Tony Butcher*

The third and final series of Merchant Navy class locomotives 35021 - 35030 were all built after Nationalisation complete with wedge-shaped cabs from new and T.I.A. water treatment equipment. In September 1949, 35021 New Zealand Line stands in Eastleigh's yard in unlined malachite green coupled to a Light Pacific tender. Brighton Works being behind time on delivering the correct 6,000-gallon tender, only then would 35021 acquire its full yellow lining. Fifteen years later and Waller's Ash tunnel near Winchester disgorges the now rebuilt 35021 New Zealand Line in September 1964.

Strathwood Library Collection & Colour Rail

Having started her career based out of Exmouth Junction when new in September 1948, a transfer to 70A Nine Elms took place in May 1951. Allowing 35021 New Zealand Line to perhaps being seen equally on both the Bournemouth and Exeter routes in her earlier years. In June 1957 she would be sent to work out of 71B Bournemouth where she would remain until her withdrawal on 8 August 1965, perhaps making her more of rarity after 1957 beyond Salisbury. Rebuilt in June 1959 she covered 859,661 miles during her working life. As we touched on earlier, some locomotives appear to be rarer photographically than others, it must be said she was one of these as we see her arriving at Southampton Central just weeks before she was taken out of traffic. *Strathwood Library Collection*

Our last view of 35021 New Zealand Line also dates from her final days, this time working the 13.30 Waterloo to Weymouth through Winchfield cutting on 4 June 1965. Four months later she would arrive at the premises of Bird's of Bridgend who would finish her off for good. The previous year had already seen 35001/2/6/9/15/18 & 35025 all withdrawn, with 1965 also claiming her sister's numbers; 35004/5/16/19/20 and 35024, things were starting to get serious!
Strathwood Library Collection

Although entering service in October 1948, 35022 Holland America Line ran with its nameplates covered over until officially named at Southampton Docks on 24 January 1949. We see her in unlettered but lined malachite green before her repaint into British Railway's lined blue in the summer of 1950, firstly blowing off furiously at Exmouth Junction and then snaking into Templecombe. One of the modifications made by Jarvis after Bulleid had left the Southern was the lowering of the boiler pressure from 280psi to 250psi.

Both: Strathwood Library Collection

One note of prestige perhaps for 35022 Holland America Line in this portrait view taken outside the testing plant at Rugby having completed its performance testing on 16 May 1952. Was that Oliver Vaughan Snell Bulleid's original design could certainly hold its own against the top link locomotives from his rivals. *Rail Archive Stephenson*

Opposite: Nonetheless, something had to be done about their shortfalls, with 35022 Holland America Line becoming the fourth of her class to be rebuilt when released in June 1956. Younger spotters respectfully stand back as she sweeps through Clapham Junction on 18 August 1957 heading for the Dorset coast. *Tony Butcher*

Almost eight years after her rebuild and 35022 Holland America Line looks better presented than in our previous view as she takes in the late winter sunshine outside Nine Elms shed on 6 March 1965, proudly displaying her 70G Weymouth shed code. The weather looks a lot fresher later the same year as she stands ready to head this special away from Waterloo on 3 October. She performed admirably on both the out and back 172-mile runs to Exeter, where she met up with Standard Class 4MTs 80039 & 80043 who performed the onward runs to Ilfracombe and Torrington before handing back to the Merchant Navy Pacific.
Rail Photoprints
& Strathwood Library Collection

Of the thirty strong class only 35011 General Steam Navigation, 35014 Nederland Line and 35023 Holland-Afrika Line seen here at Nine Elms in the early 1950s did not receive the lined blue livery variation, instead they went straight from malachite green into British Railway's lined green. Compare this view at Nine Elms of 35023 Holland-Afrika Line in her final condition just before being rebuilt during January and released back once again into traffic on 9 February 1957, against her at Exmouth Junction on 5 July 1957 once more dressed for the ACE shows the full transformation. Jarvis had sought to retain all the good points from the original Bulleid design, which was a large portion indeed, and to remove only what was considered as bad. Not all these *improvements* were well regarded by footplate crews, such as the new screw reverser and the loss of the power operated firehole doors.
Photos: Rail Archive Stephenson & R.C. Riley/The Transport Treasury

Bournemouth shed have sent out 35023 Holland-Afrika Line to work out as far as Oxford and back home again with the Manchester to Bournemouth, Pines Express routed away from the Somerset & Dorset and now via Reading. Here we see her going well near Mortimer heading south on 13 November 1965. Note how the nameplate unusually carries a hyphen. **Photos:** *Strathwood Library Collection & Gerald T. Robinson*

The neat lines of the rebuilt Merchant Navy Class Pacifics are clearly defined in this lovely, panned view taken on the Didcot East Avoiding Line as 35023 Holland-Afrika Line gets a further run out to Oxford and back with another inter-regional express during August 1964. The fireman having already attended to his duties very well judging from the gentle feather from the safety valves can relax a while and enjoy the ride, well for now at least. Being one of the earlier rebuilds from 1957, she managed over ten years of service in this form upon withdrawal in July 1967, consequently she covered 73.660 more service miles than she did in her original condition. In all she mastered 941,326 miles before being despatched from the dump at Salisbury to Buttigieg's at Newport in the early spring of 1968 for scrapping. *Rail Photoprints*

In this view the painters at Eastleigh Works even hand painted the new British Railway's crest on the tender as the transfers had yet to become available and unique in being turned out in dark blue including her wheels with crimson lining stripes with yellow Gill Sans numbers. This photograph was dated as 2 February 1949, it appears that this livery on 35024 East Asiatic Company only lasted a matter of days as she was turned out soon afterwards in what for a short time at least became the standard lined blue livery as seen below at Exmouth Junction on 9 August 1949. Notice in the top view that the battens to hold the Devon Belle boards are absent.
Colour Rail & Strathwood Library Collection

We next see 35024 East Asiatic Company passing Wilton Junction on the approach to Salisbury with an up service after her repaint into British Railways lined green livery which took place in June 1951. *Rail Photoprints*

The rebuilt self-weighing tender no.3343 with its cross-mounted style of vacuum tanks shows up well in this view taken at Nine Elms. It was paired to 35024 East Asiatic Company from 14 May 1958 and stayed with her through her rebuild in April 1959 until being swapped to no.3346 a 6,000-gallon tender on 21 December 1961. *Colour Rail*

Opposite: We see the fireman drawing a refill of water onboard 35024 East Asiatic Company for the seventy-nine-mile dash to Waterloo from here at Southampton Central with this service from Weymouth during 1962, before the chaos of the station's rebuilding a few years later. *Rail Photoprints*

Left: As 35024 East Asiatic Company sets off from Southampton Central after the stop on the previous page, we can see the more common layout of the vacuum tanks in line with the boiler, along with the substantial steel cover to make it easier for footplatemen clambering about whilst filling their tenders with water and trimming the coal. The smaller filler cap is for the T.I.A. water treatment. *Rail Photoprints*

Opposite: The enamelled centre decoration on this side at least for 35024 East Asiatic Company has seen better days. The locomotive was named in a ceremony at Waterloo six months into its service life on 5 May 1949 by HRH Prince Axel of Denmark who was Chairman of the shipping line. Upon withdrawal on 24 January 1965, the locomotive was held at Eastleigh pending removal to Messrs I.C. Woodfield in Newport who cut her up later in the year. *Rail Photoprints*

Running with her Brocklebank Line nameplates covered up as 35025 from new in November 1948 until 20 September 1949, we find the malachite green liveried Pacific getting away from Southampton Central most likely a few weeks before the naming ceremony which was carried at Waterloo. Crewed this time by Exmouth Junction men the now recently ex-works British Railway's lined green liveried 35025 Brocklebank Line sets out from Exeter Central on 14 August 1952. There would be a crew change at Salisbury with the locomotive working all the way through to Waterloo. *Both: Rail Photoprints*

Although the blue livery combined with blood & custard coaches perhaps looked great when fresh, the paint schemes wore badly in service. Demonstrated here with 35025 Brocklebank Line at Dover just before her repaint into a sparking lined green livery seen spick and span ex-works at Eastleigh in July 1952. *Both: Strathwood Library Collection*

Another visit to Surbiton in November 1957 to record the passing of the down Bournemouth Belle, today hauled by 35025 Brocklebank Line which has had those once elegant front flares around the buffer beam now removed during a previous routine visit to Eastleigh Works. *Tony Butcher*

Soon after 35025 Brocklebank Line was rebuilt in December 1956, she visited Swindon Works during July and August the following year for assessment on their stationary test plant, this was after a report of a knock within her motion. The solution was found, and suitable modifications were made to all the rebuilds thereafter. There appears to be nothing now troubling the running 35025 Brocklebank Line as she speeds through the outer London suburbs towards Waterloo around 1962. Very soon the Southern Region would be hit hard with a mass cull of steam locomotives. The end would come for this Merchant Navy Pacific on 7 September 1964 being set aside in the goods yard at Exmouth Junction. Fortune would smile upon her now as she was purchased by Woodham's of Barry where she would remain until February 1986. Restoration for this example is proving to be a long and dedicated road for the preservationists. **Photos: Strathwood Library Collection & Colour Rail**

Being among the first of the class to enter service during 1948 at a time when there was a great deal of uncertainty about locomotive liveries, 35026 Lamport & Holt Line made her debut on 4 December in a plain unlined malachite green, until being painted into the then standard British Railways lined blue livery chosen for the class in the summer of 1949. By the summer of 1953 she was running in lined British Railway's green livery as we see her approaching Shortlands Junction with the 11.00 Victoria - Dover Marine Golden Arrow prestige service on 11 July. Although originally fitted with 5,500-gallon tenders 35021 – 35030 were retro fitted with 6,000-gallon tenders to assist footplate crews to make the 108-mile run from Waterloo to Bournemouth non-stop, the redundant 5,500-gallon tenders then being paired to Light Pacifics. These larger water capacity tenders were also 16 inches longer in their wheelbase. With the end of steam getting ever closer, enthusiast tours took locomotives further and further afield such as on 22 October 1966 where 35026 Lamport & Holt Line draws a crowd as she is topped up for the return run from here at Newcastle Central to York.
Both: Rail Photoprints

Another such northern jaunt for 35026 Lamport & Holt Line a few weeks later 20 November 1966 which took her on a round trip from Manchester Piccadilly to York and back. Heading out via Sheffield and Doncaster then returning via Normanton and Huddersfield, certainly not regular ground for a Weymouth allocated Pacific. All the windows were occupied as enthusiasts have a look to see what the trouble is perhaps at a signal stop here at Disley, hopefully nothing wrong. In fact, there would thirteen enthusiast rail tours that year that included Merchant Navy haulage as part of their itineraries. Those locomotives participating included 35011/23/26 & 35028, remarkably 35011 General Steam Navigation managed both her tours in the first two days of January for she was withdrawn on 6 February. The other four examples would survive into 1967, with 35026 Lamport & Holt Line being the next of this group to go. Set aside on 26 March 1967 at her home shed of Weymouth, she would depart for Cashmore's yard in Newport on 5 August on a journey that would take several weeks including stopovers such as this one at Gloucester.

Photos: Rail Photoprints & Strathwood Library Collection

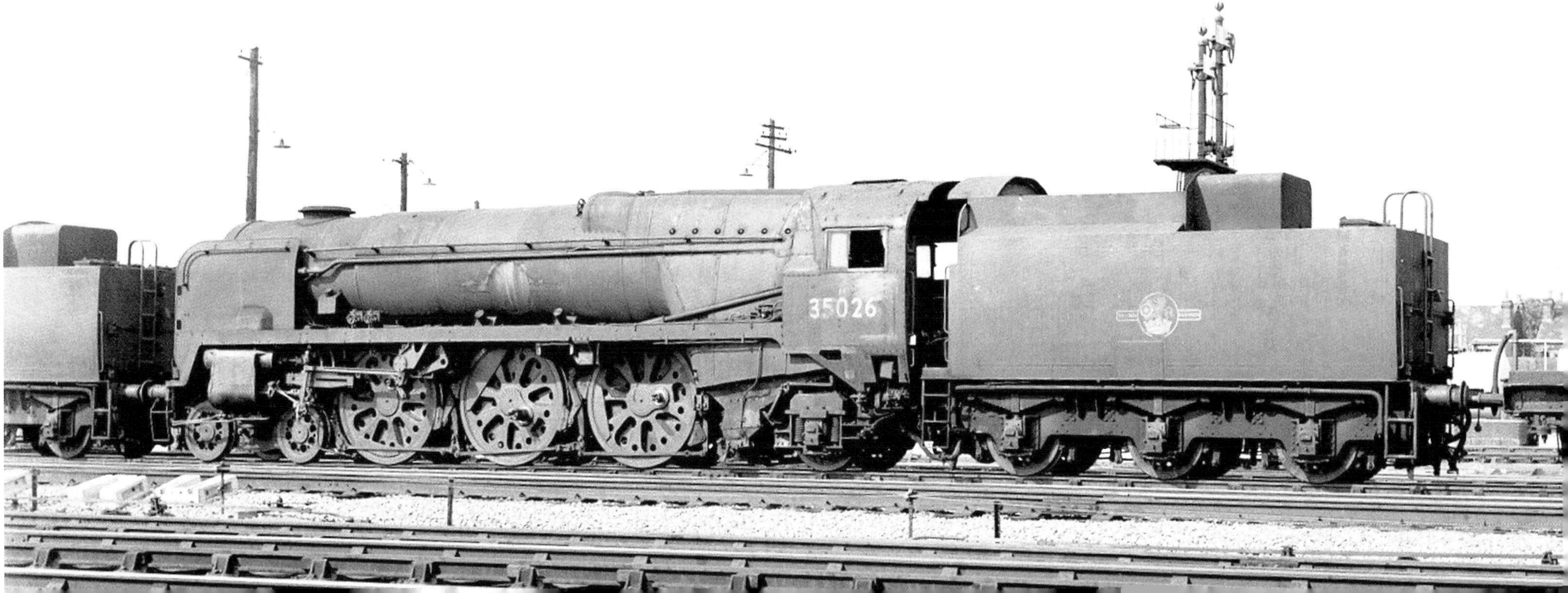

Although these two photographs suggest the opposite about the early liveries on the class, the light blue livery with black and white lining as seen on 35027 Port Line with her full Golden Arrow departing from Victoria during 1950 with her cylinder drain cocks open, looks splendid. Sadly, this adventurous newly applied paint scheme did not wear so well in regular service and as a result was relatively short-lived. She would be painted into lined green as part of her next light intermediate overhaul within Eastleigh Works during the autumn of 1953. We next see her after transfer back to the Western Section now based at Bournemouth from the summer of 1955 until her demise. Here at Nine Elms, she looks much grubbier as her freshly topped up coal supply is trimmed, also of note is the ex-MoD brake van S35106 acquired by the LSWR after WW1 in the background.
Photos: C.R.L. Coles/Rail Archive Stephenson & Rail Online

The once spotless appearance after her rebuilding in May 1957 seems far behind her now as 35027 Port Line speeds the heavy Pullman stock making up the down Bournemouth Belle through Berrylands, on her way back to her home shed, standards have definitely slipped further. The nameplate's lower infill support shows well in this view along with the oily sand build-up so typical of the class during their final years. She was another of the class to run more mileage in her rebuilt guise than beforehand, with 508,939 afterwards and just 363,351 beforehand. Being another of the Woodham's success stories for preservation she has happily added further to her rebuilt mileage since escaping Barry scrapyard in December 1982.
Both: Strathwood Library Collection

Opposite: We take a final look at 35027 Port Line off her normal patch on shed at Wolverhampton's Oxley shed on 26 March 1966 having hauled a football supporter's special from Southampton. She would be withdrawn from service a few months later on 18 September. Long gone was the honour and glory bestowed upon 35027 Port Line in April 1959, as the motive power for hauling the Royal Train from Windsor to Hamworthy Junction. Although she would collect one further honour in 1988 becoming the first ex-Barry Merchant Navy to return to steam. *Rail Photoprints*

Ultimately destined to be the fortunate one to be sold out of service and straight into preservation, we see 35028 Clan Line with her nameplates still covered up in what appears to be a filthy condition on shed at Stewarts Lane. She was sent out new on 23 December 1948 originally in the attractive lined malachite green. Next, she would be repainted into lined blue at Eastleigh Works a few days before being named within Southampton Docks on 15 January 1951 by Lord Rotherwick the Chairman of Clan Line. This view certainly confirms why she was repainted into blue. *The Transport Treasury*

This is more like it, although the cladding around the firebox appears to be coming away in this view of her ready to back off Stewarts Lane shed to head for Victoria one morning in March 1953. Although still in the lined blue livery, her next repaint was just a few months away as part of a heavy intermediate overhaul in the spring of 1953. Aside from being returned into service in lined green we can see she had also lost her front valances too in this view a few years later at Bournemouth Central on 17 April 1955, although she was still based at Stewarts Lane.
Photos: Rail Photoprints & R.C.T.S. Archive

One aspect of 35028 Clan Line becoming the last of her class to be rebuilt heading back into traffic on 24 October 1959, was that she managed to keep an un-modified 6,000-gallon tender complete with the later version of the British Railways emblem until being finally stopped for her rebuild on 21 August 1959. One of her last duties on the Eastern Section based out of Stewarts Lane perhaps before heading to Eastleigh might have been this down service from Victoria near Orpington that summer. Taken just a fortnight after her release from rebuilding she certainly looked the part on shed at Eastleigh on 7 November 1959 with black backed nameplates. *Photos: The Transport Library & Strathwood Library Collection*

Another view of the smooth changeover process when working westwards from Salisbury this time on 27 May 1963. The Nine Elms driver stands guard over the water crane while both the soon to be relieved fireman and his Exmouth Junction based colleague attend to the coal assisted by a local Salisbury based man. On the footplate the driver has the blower on while he attends to his oiling round the motion to satisfy himself all is well for the onwards journey home to Exeter. Just six minutes was allowed for this process in the working timetables to include perhaps as much as 5,000 gallons of water being taken on. The prominent W sign was off course to show the position of the water column for the footplate crew. But all footplatemen would know where every water column was, as part of their route knowledge. Opposite it is a much more relaxed situation prior to departure for 35028 Clan Line in this scene at Waterloo as they brew up ready for a Bournemouth line departure from London during 1964. The nameplates are now backed with red paint in both views. *Photos: Strathwood Library Collection & Rail Photoprints*

The adhesion of the yellow lining decorating 35029 Ellerman Lines appears questionable in this view at Nine Elms from most likely sometime during 1950. The nameplates remained covered from when she was new on 19 February 1949, until her naming on 1 March 1951 as the last of the class to be officially named. *Rail Archive Stephenson*

Having gone through her blue period 35029 Ellerman Lincs was repainted in the otherwise standard British Railway's lined green during a light intermediate overhaul at Eastleigh Works, except the usual style of straight lining across the cab sides was modified and her number painted somewhat lower than the norm. The same works visit in the early summer of 1952 also saw the removal of the front casing valances too. This oddball cab repaint was because 35029 Ellerman Lines was originally expected to be paired with the modified self-weighing tender, which in the end did not come to fruition. *Colour Rail*

On 1 July 1956, a visit to Bournemouth rewards us with this view of 35029 Ellerman Lines about to exit the turntable in the shed yard with her cabside now repainted as normal. Many drivers felt that these locomotives were stronger in their original condition, and that the rebuilds were slower to steam freely when the regulator was opened up. *R.C.T.S. Archive*

Opposite: The sooty face of this fireman at Exmouth Junction during June 1962 tends to confirm that the cabs of Merchant Navy Pacifics albeit extremely comfortable to ride in they were also very dusty in traffic. Another aspect of Bulleid's design was to arrange the cab so that both driver and fireman could work without getting in each other's way. *Rail Photoprints*

We can see opposite that the enamelled centre display for 35029 Ellerman Lines' nameplates certainly carried the most flags and pennants of the class. She appears to be more respectable in this later view of her at Nine Elms ready to back down to Waterloo for her next departure on 3 April 1965. This duty will almost certainly be back towards her Dorset home of Weymouth with Warship diesels now being the regulars on the services to Exeter. Withdrawn from service the week ending 11 September 1966, she would be another of the class to head for Barry scrapyard. Here she laid until "rescued" for preservation in January 1974. Although some might argue she was at least saved and that she provides an impressive sectioned educational exhibit within the National Railway Museum, while many others mourn her dismemberment. *Photos: **Strathwood Library Collection & Colour Rail***

A small gathering is on hand to watch the arrival of 35030 Elder-Dempster Lines as she draws into Basingstoke station past the shed buildings on 17 April 1957. She was the last of the class to enter service on 1 April 1949 in a lined-out malachite green livery without any lettering upon her tender and the front skirting and cylinder blocks painted black. The official naming took place within Southampton Docks on 5 June 1950, by which time she had been freshly painted into the standard British Railway's lined blue livery. As with her sisters this in turn gave way to the lined British Railway's green livery, in this instance as part of her heavy intermediate overhaul at Eastleigh in the spring of 1953. Originally sent to work on the Eastern Section she transferred to the Western Section at Nine Elms on 21 June 1955. *Tony Butcher*

Departure time will soon be upon the crew of 35030 Elder-Dempster Lines with a West of England service away from Waterloo during 1963. Although the last to be built her turn within the rebuilding program came up in April 1958 as the fifteenth to be so treated. She would not be the lowest mileage example either that dubious honour befell her direct predecessor 35029 Ellerman Lines. *Rail Photoprints*

Opposite: Good preparation was always essential before leaving Nine Elms shed for Waterloo departures. As once at the terminus they would be faced with restrictions placed upon the fireman to keep his engine both quiet, without any blowing off and free from smoke. Yet both driver and fireman would still need to be ready for the journey ahead starting with a climb away from the ex-L.S.W.R terminus, often slipping during wet weather. The fireman would be into the swing of things as they pass Clapham Junction feeding a few rounds of coal around the firebox in preparation for his driver opening her up once free of the speed restrictions as witnessed by 35030 Elder-Dempster Lines getting into her stride here at Clapham Junction on 2 January 1965. *Colour Rail*

Perhaps appropriately the last built of the class worked until the close of steam operations on the Southern Region on Sunday 9 July 1967, being seen in steam at Nine Elms on that final weekend. On 3 September she was hauled to the dump at Salisbury as the first part of heading west towards Buttigieg's scrapyard in Newport. The last leg of this final journey was eventually made on 23 March 1968. We leave our coverage of the Merchant Navies with a fine shed shot from around 1965 on a calm and still evening at Eastleigh from that master exponent of nocturnal portraits and Patricroft footplateman Jim Carter. *Rail Online*

The Powerful and Brutish Q1s

Destined for preservation as part of the National Collection, perhaps in recognition of the importance of Bulleid's design, 70C Guildford's 33001 keeps mixed company on shed at Reading during early April 1964, less than six weeks from being withdrawn.
Strathwood Library Collection

Much has been written criticised about what was Bulleid's perhaps most successful design. Having taken charge of the Southern Railway's motive power upon the retirement of Maunsell joining a railway with aspirations towards electrification of its predominantly passenger orientated routes in 1937, he inherited several existing locomotive building and electrification programs upon taking office. If we couple the expectations no doubt of the Southern Railway's management board along with the effects from previous years of the Great Depression of the 1930s, at the same time also running straight into the country going to war in September 1939, we should perhaps cut the great man some slack.

It was soon realised that the prospects of perhaps building a further batch of forty of Maunsell's Q Class 0-6-0s, was not to be the answer to reduce the probability of being forced to double head the massively increased weights of freight trains now running on the Southern. Likewise, shortages of steel and other raw materials to continue building further of Stanier's Class 8F 2-8-0s for war use, sent Riddles back to the drawing board to produce a similar powerful design using far less and more economic materials. Similarly, Bulleid surmised that the Southern Railway really needed an almost superpowered 0-6-0 with a superior route availability over any of the much heavier 2-8-0 or even 2-10-0 designs.

The result would be in the form of Bulleid's forty strong Class Q1 0-6-0 locomotives, his remarkable design brought about an average of 20% more horsepower over other modern for their time 0-6-0 types from the big four, such as Collett's 2251, Fowler's 4F, Gresley's J39 and Maunsell's Q Class. Not only that the weight of material savings across a total of forty of Bulleid's Q1 locomotives against say that of the latter Maunsell design, was 14tons less per locomotive, equal to a massive 700tons of raw materials across the whole class, at a time when every ton mattered dearly.

Originally designed with a just a short-term function in mind, the forty strong class went on to last unscathed by withdrawals for twenty-one years. Again, keeping company with a Standard Class 4MT, 33002 takes a rest at Eastbourne at the start of the sixties surrounded by the shattered remains of the former L.B.S.C.R. engine shed which suffered much war damage from the Luftwaffe. Likewise, Nine Elms was in the thick of it too in the capital. The original black-out shutters on the tender show up well on 33003 on shed at 70A on 20 August 1961. *Colour Rail & Strathwood Library Collection*

Left: Guildford's 33003 takes a rest in the shed yard at Eastleigh on 16 May 1959, she would soon take up residence on the Eastern Section instead with her new allocation to Tonbridge the following month. *R.C.T.S. Archive*

Opposite: The lack of braking ability for the Q1s meant they were restricted to normally not working west of Salisbury because of Honiton's bank, with only very few exceptions limiting their loads. Nonetheless here we see Feltham's 33004 approaching Salisbury with a westbound goods on 8 June 1963. *Gerald T. Robinson*

A chance to have its fire and ash cleaned along with a fresh load of coal the hard and dirty way alongside the rather basic facilities that existed at 70C Guildford. Having been sent new here in June 1942, 33005 was based here all her twenty-one-year working life, save for a couple of months in 1953. *Tony Butcher*

Opposite: Although 33006 seems to have got around quite a bit in later years and appeared on several rail tours, perhaps her spiritual home was 70B Feltham being allocated here for over fourteen years across two spells, aside from a short stint at Three Bridges she was otherwise allocated to Guildford or Nine Elms often bringing her back here almost daily. On 13 May 1961 she was out of steam at Feltham for a washout when caught broadside photographically. A general overhaul at Ashford Works ten months previously had seen her fitted with AWS and water treatment equipment, the latter denoted by the yellow triangle under her cab side number. The two larger access holes for the lower washout plugs were progressively retro fitted to class members as they passed through works from around 1953. *Jim Oatway*

Right: By the start of 1966 there were just three of the class left in traffic, spending most of their final months of the previous year working permanent way trains in connection with the Bournemouth electrification. Officially the last three 33006, 33020 and 33027 were all withdrawn during January 1966 from 70C Guildford. Although 33006 now complete with a 70A Nine Elms shed plate was returned from the dead to work several legs of the LCGB's New Forrester Rail Tour, as here on 19 March at Gosport. Then one last fling for the class when she shared the final leg of the LCGB's Wilts & Hants Rail Tour with U Class 31639 from Salisbury to Waterloo, taking the "Cook's tour" route via Romsey, Southampton Central, Eastleigh, Alton and Woking on 3 April 1966. All that was left was to be dragged to Cashmore's scrapyard in Newport with a stopover at Gloucester during July and August 1966. *George Woods*

Many of the class were given the newer style of British Railways emblem during overhauls or works repairs mainly at Ashford although Eastleigh conducted a few repairs post-1957, both larger and smaller versions were used, modellers beware! A further view at Salisbury brings us 33007 taking a gentle canter through the station light engine in August 1963, having arrived in the city from her home at Feltham on a goods train earlier. Her demise would come just four months later in January at her home shed in south-west London before lingering a further ten months dumped in the yard awaiting passage to Cashmore's in Newport. *Rail Photoprints*

Other workings for these Bulleid 0-6-0s included ecs and pilot duties, such as with another of Feltham's long term Q1 residents 33008 seen at Basingstoke on 22 July 1962. Withdrawn the week ending 25 August a year later, she would be dragged up the Midland mainline along with some other scrappers from Feltham to George Cohen's yard at Cransley near Kettering during March 1964. *Chris Wilson Collection*

Meanwhile, 33009 also from Feltham takes a refill of water during her break at Waterloo the following year having worked in tender first from Clapham Junction with ecs. Both locomotives on this page having been retro-fitted with mechanical lubricators connected to the front driving wheels.
Strathwood Library Collection

Passenger work for 33009 on Thursday 9 July 1953 as she takes the Hounslow line at Barnes with an excursion from the Eastern Region. At this point her mechanical lubricator was still to be fitted. *The Bluebell Museum Archive*

On 6 June 1959, it was empty stock duties for 33010 as she seems to be going well through Earlsfield. At higher speeds above 50mph they tended to rock and roll a bit and the tenders vibrated excessively. Part of the reason for this was to keep the locomotive's weight down and to save on valuable steel when they were built insufficient baffles and strengthening were used. It was reported that some of these issues which also led to water leaks were later repaired with extra steel being welded in and several inches of concrete being poured into the bottom of the tender in an attempt to bolster matters up. In doing so it was also thought that by increasing the weight in the tender, it might make a modest improvement to the locomotive's braking ability.
Strathwood Library Collection

Above. It's a spell of passenger work for 33011 across the North Downs near Gomshall and Shere on 17 May 1962. When withdrawn during August 1963, she had missed out completely on being fitted with both a mechanical lubricator or AWS. Her final resting place would be Eastleigh Works two months later. **Colour Rail**

Further examples of Feltham's use of the class on cross-London freight workings, as we see 33012 standing in the London Midland Region's Brent Yard near Cricklewood during 1952. Cast an eye to the front of the locomotive's chimney which has begun to rust through what was no doubt second rate steel from wartime production. **Alec Swain/The Transport Treasury**

Similarly, 33013 has ventured across town having just passed under the former Great Eastern Railway's route to Cambridge near Graham Road. Although sent brand new to Eastleigh in October 1942, she moved to Guildford in November 1947 before beginning a long-term association with Feltham in April 1948 that would last until withdrawn on 7 July 1963. *Rail Archive Stephenson*

In the months straight after Nationalisation in 1948, there was confusion for the painters upon the new policy for renumbering locomotives, the first of the Q1s were dealt with using the previous Bulleid sunshine style, whereas some retained Southern on their tenders while others were marked up with British Railways, once again in the previous sunshine style. This is 33014 as running the following year on 17 April 1949 on shed at Eastleigh. In typical latter-day condition 33015 takes a turn on the turntable to access all the shed roads here at 70C Guildford in July 1964, another bastion for the class.
Both: Strathwood Library Collection

A clearer view of the mechanical lubricator fitted to 33016 while taking water on what must be a cold day at Nine Elms on 17 March 1962, as the young fireman has climbed back into the warmth of the cab wearing his gloves. *R.C.T.S. Archive*

Opposite: Preparation time for 33017 at Bournemouth on 28 July 1960 for its next run back home towards 70A Nine Elms, as another of the class looks on in the background. Withdrawn from Three Bridges on 5 January 1964, she would become another of the eleven Q1s to be cut up at Eastleigh Works. *Colour Rail*

A short-lived experiment appears on 33018 at Ashford shed most likely just after its heavy intermediate overhaul within the nearby works during May and June 1949. We can see an alternative arrangement of handrail for the unfortunate souls tasked with sweeping out the smokebox being considered, obviously not the solution. *Colour Rail*

Earlier days on the former S.E.C.R.'s Redhill route from here at Reading South on 3 November 1956 sees 33019 making a storming departure for back home at Guildford.
R.C. Riley/The Transport Treasury

Remarkably none of the Q1s were caught in the great cull of Southern Region steam locomotives at the end of 1962, however by the close of 1963 their forty-strong number had been reduced to twenty-seven examples. The following year took out another twenty leaving just seven to begin 1965. As a result, they were now in demand for rail tour use, such as 33020 top and tailing with 33027 along the Lavant branch from Chichester with the L.C.G.B.'s Vectis Farewell Rail Tour on 3 October 1965. Both engines would run for short while longer and then the pair would both head to Buttigieg's in Newport for scrap as the only two broken up in this yard. *Gerald T. Robinson*

A few years beforehand 33020 saw her last visit to Eastleigh Works who took over repairs from Ashford. This view recording her was taken ex-works ready to resume service after this heavy intermediate overhaul which had begun on 8 March and was completed on 13 April 1963. She proudly displays her 71A shed code as an Eastleigh engine where she spent most of her working life. Note that the cover for the clack valves has been left off. *Strathwood Library Collection*

Opposite: The missing panels situation was not just an end of steam thing as seen by 33021 at Bournemouth on 21 April 1956. Construction for the class was carried out simultaneously during 1942 between Brighton Works with numbers C1 to C16 and Ashford Works with C17 to C36, leaving Brighton to chip in again with C37 to C40, all using Bulleid's continental style of numbering with C denoting six coupled wheels. *R.C.T.S. Archive*

Several prospective passengers are on hand to greet 33022 into Sandhurst Halt station in July 1963 on the Reading to Redhill route. Note the colour light signalling but there is still only gas lighting for the station. *Colour Rail*

Certainly, powerful enough for the job at hand, 33023 heads a lengthy down freight through Broadstone on 21 September 1959 as a regular turn for this Eastleigh based engine. *Rail Archive Stephenson*

Home for 33024 from November 1953 until her transfer to Feltham in February 1961, was 74D Tonbridge where we see her comfortably at rest outside the shed on 24 May 1958. This would be another of the class to miss out on being fitted with a mechanical lubricator before being withdrawn it seems. *Rail Archive Stephenson*

Opposite: Employment today is on behalf of the civil engineers for 33025 as she draws a rake of ballast wagons originating from Meldon Quarry in Devon through Guildford station on a splendid day in May 1960. She would also be among the early casualties withdrawn in July 1963, as such was another of those cut up at Eastleigh Works. *Colour Rail*

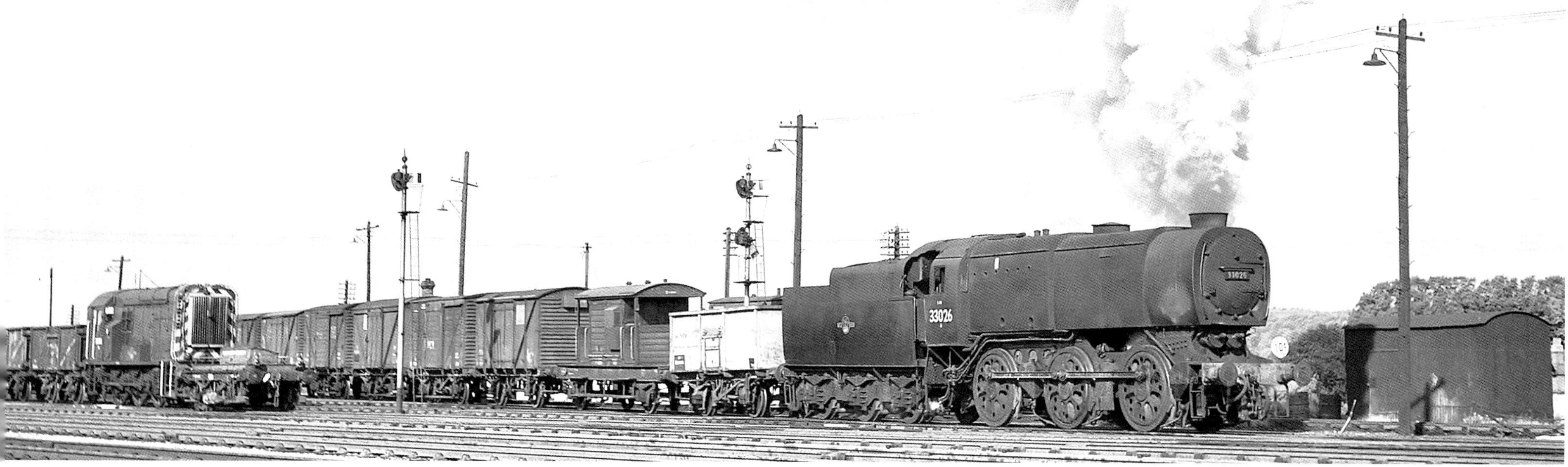

Not withdrawn until 26 September 1965, 33026 impressively leaves Scours Lane Sidings, Reading with a freight train to the Southern on 10 October 1964. *Gerald T. Robinson*

Below: Being prepared alongside the running shed at Feltham on 11 February 1964 we can see the AWS equipment beneath the cab's footplate and how the crew were both protected against the weather and the glare from the locomotive's fire from above during the Second World War. *Colour Rail*

Piloted by C Class 31004, the fireman of 33028 glances down at his injector feeds as they run through Ham Street & Orlestone on 6 August 1961. The Q1 still carries the original yellow circle denoting water softening equipment is fitted, before it was changed to a yellow triangle so as not to clash with the Western Region's route classification. She would be the first of the class to be withdrawn with a cracked cylinder on 3 January 1963. *Colour Rail*

Opposite: A dubious last honour for Tonbridge's 33029 at the closure of the Westerham branch from the mainline at Dunton Green on 28 October 1961. With the rundown of steam activity and closure of both branch lines and goods facilities throughout Kent and East Sussex, 33029 headed first to south west London to join the fray at Feltham briefly at the end of May 1962, before taking up her final residence at Three Bridges after 22 October 1962. Withdrawal here came early in 1964 on 5 January where she remained until 6 June heading for Eastleigh, thence to Bird's of Morriston in Swansea via Gloucester during mid-July for scrap.
Colour Rail

An interesting aerial view looking down upon 33030 also from Three Bridges shed shuffling around the shed yard at Brighton next to the seaside resort's station on 28 June 1963. Alongside the diminutive Terrier in service as the shed pilot shunts a disabled Class 08 diesel shunter past an equally lame Class 04 being repaired.
Ian Nolan

The boiler washout plug holes have been numbered in chalk on 33030 after her recent stop for attention here at Feltham to be sure they go back correctly when seen on 13 April 1962. *Jim Oatway*

Opposite: Having picked up an inter-regional freight working at Didcot, Feltham's 33030 passes through Tilehurst station with a working back to the Southern Region and Feltham's once large marshalling yard on 8 February 1964. *Gerald T. Robinson*

The driver of 33031 eases his featherweight load through Ashford on 27 August 1960 having been signalled to do so from this gantry sited higher than usual in order to be seen above the footbridge in the background by approaching trains. *Colour Rail*

Our next view is in fact taken from the footbridge seen in the background on the previous page, as this time it is another Tonbridge based locomotive, 33032 arriving at Ashford past the town's cattle market on 16 February 1960. *Colour Rail*

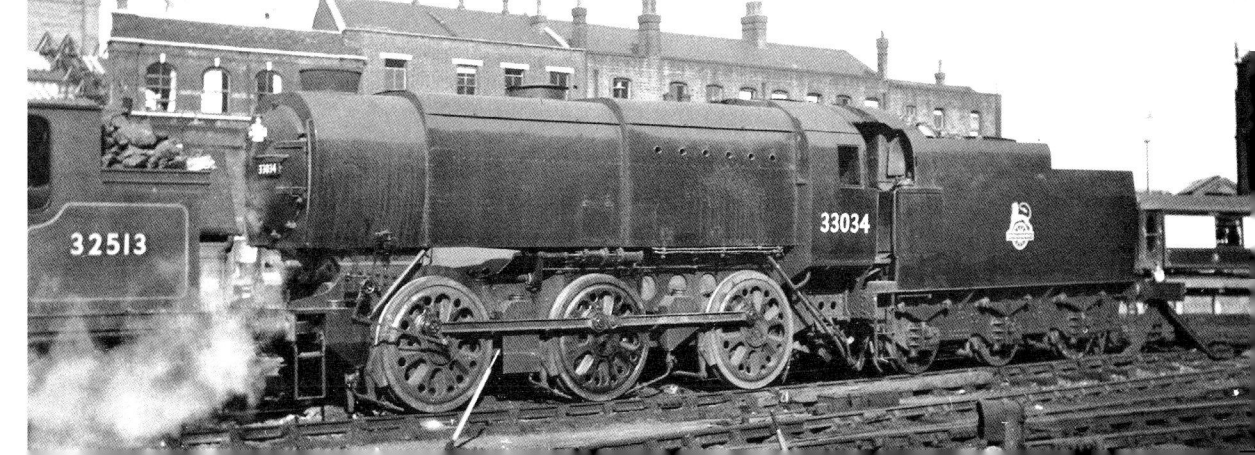

Left: This shot of 33033 on shed at Reading most likely dates from early 1964 just before the locomotive was withdrawn from Guildford on 14 June 1964. *Rail Online*

We believe this undated shot of 33034 from Tonbridge shed was taken at Brighton soon after its recent heavy casual overhaul at Ashford Works in the final months of 1954. Although as a Guildford based engine when withdrawn on 5 January 1964, she was placed into storage at Fratton shed until being made ready to travel dead to Bird's of Morriston in July the same year. **Rail Online**

Opposite: Enthusiasts and staff scurry around a very sodden Bordon station to keep out of the rain yet still photograph 33035 while working the Railway Enthusiast Club's Hampshire Hog rail tour on 14 March 1964, at least one wise gent has come prepared, well done sir. Bordon station had closed to passenger traffic on 16 September 1957 and the branch remained open for goods only until 3 April 1966. Sadly 33035 did not last much longer after this rail tour as she was withdrawn just three months later on 14 June. She would become one of the seven Q1s to be cut up at King's of Norwich, the others being 33003/23/30/33/39 & 33040. *Rail Photoprints*

It's Whit Monday, 21 May 1956 and it has been a lovely warm bank holiday, but it is now drawing to a close as we see 33036 come off the Sidley Viaduct heading for Bexhill West with the 17.52 from Tonbridge service. Not so many passengers on this train, however the return working will most likely justify the number of coaches as folk head home after a pleasant day out at the seaside, simple pleasures. The branch swung off the Hastings mainline at Crowhurst and found itself part of the Beeching axe being closed on 15 June 1964. By then now allocated to 70C Guildford, 33036 was also withdrawn a fortnight later on the 28th. *The Bluebell Museum Archive*

Opposite: Another casualty from the Eastern Section would be 33037 transferred away from Tonbridge to here at Eastleigh on 26 May 1961. Although a Feltham engine when new, after 1 April 1948 she then rotated through several sheds including Stewarts Lane, Tonbridge, Stewarts Lane, Hither Green, Brighton, back once more to Hither Green before landing again at Tonbridge in May 1959. Was she a bad 'en, perhaps? This view was taken on 9 September 1961, Eastleigh it seems lost patience with her too and withdrew her on 6 October 1963 and promptly cut her up with a couple of weeks. *R.C.T.S. Archive*

Still looking smart at Eastleigh on 2 March 1963 was 33038 visiting from Feltham, her last works visit here had been four months earlier for a light casual. It would be her last of course and it was most likely when the meaty looking patch was applied to her leaking tender tank too. Feltham kept her in traffic until 5 January 1964, when she made her way back here to Eastleigh for cutting up just weeks later. Born out of necessity and certainly looking way different to just about anything before them, the Q1s picked up several nicknames, such as Charlies, Coffee Pots, Warthogs and Utilities. *Peter Simmonds*

Opposite: On 4 September 1956, 33039 from Tonbridge has pulled up at Ham Street & Orleston with this goods service conveniently for our cameraman. *Colour Rail*

The signals are off for a down express as 33040 gets away from Ashford with a heavy down goods on 28 July 1960 heading home towards Tonbridge. *Colour Rail*

The strange shape of the boiler cladding and sheeting on Bulleid's Q1 came about by his use of a lightweight fibreglass insulation called Idaglass, instead of the traditional asbestos based cladding. This view of 33040 at Ashford Works during an overhaul in 1960 shows the two support sections required to hold the steel boiler cladding up as the Idaglass insulation could not support any weight itself. The absence of a traditional running plate in the design shows how large the sand boxes were and being low down that they at least would be convenient to replenish at engine sheds. The middle ones having a plate welded to their base to avoid men catching their feet when standing on the connecting rod. *Colour Rail*

And Now for Something Completely Different

Originally painted black by Brighton Works, 36001 was the first of what became known as the Leader Class arrived here at Eastleigh hauled by one of Billington's K Class Moguls on 26 June 1949. It was hurriedly repainted into a silver/grey livery and given the then brand-new British Railways "cycling lion" emblems amidships, see overleaf. *Colour Rail*

The whole concept of this revolutionary project arose in December 1944 as the Southern Railway wanted to consider something to replace their aging Drummond Class M7 0-4-4Ts. Bulleid suggested that a much more powerful mixed traffic design would be a better solution as a replacement, perhaps even further batches of his Q1 0-6-0s might be suitable. During the following year suggestions that a tank locomotive design might more desirable were dismissed as the Southern had a previous bad experience with the fatal derailment at Sevenoaks of a Maunsell designed 2-6-4T in 1927. In the style of his Q1 locomotives, Bulleid proposed 0-6-2T and 0-6-4T designs and a massive 4-6-4T as well as the double ended 0-6-6-0T design we know now as the Leader.

The Southern's general manager Sir Eustace Missenden decreed that Bulleid should commence with the construction of five locomotives to his drawing W7236 (the Leader). Considering the time towards the close of World War Two, it was to be a brave new world as the LMS was moving towards their own diesel traction ideas with 10000 and 10001, the LNER wanted to complete their Woodhead 1500v dc plans from before the hostilities and the GWR mooted gas turbine power as the way forward.

So, the concept of a futuristic steam locomotive was not so radical maybe after all. Meanwhile of course Bulleid had proposed and built his first two electric Co-Co locomotives for the Central Section.

As the cost of electrifying the Western Section was way beyond the possibilities of the day, the board's choice was steam. With construction to be at Brighton Works, by 22 June 1949 the first locomotive 36001 was complete and made a very brief run from the works to the station before unfortunately failing. Further testing a few days later was abandoned this time at Groombridge as the new locomotive's water filler was too high for the water columns available.

The greatest issue was that Bulleid had decided as he had also done with his Pacifics and the Q1s beforehand, to incorporate just about every new design and idea he could think of within the project.

A view from the station footbridge at Guildford shows 36001 being attended to by fitters before heading back to Brighton on another test run, no doubt for further head scratching as to how can we get this to work more reliably?
Strathwood Library Collection

Two views of 36001 at Eastleigh during 1950 with a team of fitters never far away. Between 22 June 1949 and 2 February 1950, 36001 managed to work seventy trial runs from Brighton to Oxted and Crowborough around 80 miles or perhaps out and back to Eastleigh for 120 miles. Oliver Bulleid had already left the Southern Region of British Railways in September 1949 to become a consultant engineer to the CIE in Ireland. Modifications were still being made by Eastleigh Works as required, with a regular footplate crew employed so lessons were learned from each trip out. Trials were to include drawbar tests and speed as well although limited to just 50mph. Further testing was planned to extend into the autumn of 1950, when Robin Riddles' deputy Roland Bond was due to attend a test run to Basingstoke with a decent 450 plus ton load. Things started well but as ever ended with further problems. Finally, on 20 November, Robin Riddles had heard enough and condemned the whole project in a memo.

Sensibly, Brighton Works had already halted further construction on 36003 to 36005, whereas 36002 had also been robbed of parts such as its crank axles to keep 36001 mobile for testing. Even before the Leader project was finally abandoned both 36002 and 36003 had been shuffled away into storage, firstly at New Cross Gate where we see the former, and later to the disused engine shed at Bognor Regis just before it was demolished. The fate of 36001 was to be first being dumped at Eastleigh before heading to Brighton Works for dismantling inside the main workshops along with 36002 & 36003. The frames for 36004 & 36005 having already been dismantled for scrap. By now the press had acquired the full story, with the Sunday Dispatch pulling no punches whatsoever on 18 January 1953, as they used the whole episode of Bulleid's Leader project to criticise the nationalised railway system's use of public funds.

Photos: Strathwood Library Collection

Being shunted into Brighton Works for the final time during 1951, the works' Terrier shunter 377S musters its strength to shove the estimated 130ton weight of 36001 away from the public's gaze and ready for breaking up. *Rail Online*

Opposite: The uncompleted hulk that was to have become 36003 was recorded for all to see as they arrived and departed from Brighton on 22 May 1951, before it too was discreetly disposed of inside the works. *The Bluebell Museum Archive*

Creative Thinking

Opposite: Bulleid also applied his creative thinking towards improving existing locomotives from his predecessors. Such as overseeing that twenty-one of the Schools Class were fitted with Lemaitre multiple-jet blast pipes with much wider chimneys to improve their draughting such as 30929 Malvern seen here at Bricklayers Arms. The results while advantageous were not enough to justify the whole class to be so treated. Likewise, Urie King Arthurs such as 30737 King Uther enjoyed similar treatment.

Photos: Strathwood Library Collection & Rail Photoprints

A Bulleid "bucket" style chimney was applied as part of the modifications to the Marsh designed Class H1 32039 Hartland Point which was converted as a test bed in September 1947 for the Leader project. This involved fitting it with sleeve valves operated by levers, it was converted to be chain driven by sprockets attached to the centre driving axle. To manage this, it required the creative use of a replacement front bogie taken from a Billington Class D3 0-4-4T. The warning signs for the Leader project were there already as 32039 in this modified form only ran test trains as her water consumption was described as prolific.

Strathwood Library Collection

Opposite: Multiple-jet blastpipes and large diameter chimneys certainly improved the performance of all twenty of the Maunsell designed Q Class 0-6-0s as they were regarded as poor steamers as built. After a time though, corrosion was found to be a problem which resulted in seven of the class being fitted with new British Railways standard single chimneys, and one with an ugly stove-pipe chimney. This one 30546 seen at Eastleigh making smoke after being lit up kept its distinctive Bulleid embellishment until withdrawn in May 1964. *Colour Rail*

Another of Maunsell's designs to benefit from some Bulleid thinking were the sixteen members of the Lord Nelson Class of 4-6-0s. From 1938 onwards their cylinders and tenders were modified as they were also fitted with multiple-jet blast pipes, large chimneys and smoke deflectors. Here we see 30857 Lord Howe still putting these improvements to good use heading south from Clapham Junction in March 1962. *Peter Simmonds*

In the same way as his predecessor Richard Maunsell had done Oliver Bulleid was also to apply himself to more modern forms of traction and coaching stock. Perhaps his most creative were the two double-decked four-car units built in an attempt to solve increased passenger loading issues, against the physical problems of extending the platforms all along the Dartford route to accommodate longer ten-car trains which would otherwise be required during the peak periods. Great idea in principle but flawed in practice as they were uncomfortable and slower in both loading and unloading at stations.
David Brown Collection

To provide additional units for the electrification to Gillingham and Maidstone and a later need for increasing the Reading line services to eight cars from six, Bulleid went for this design classified as a 2-HAL. The distinctive frontal form of this leading unit seen at Beckenham Junction in 1958 was repeated on ten 4-SUB units and two additional 4-LAV units he also commissioned.
David Brown Collection

Another of his trademark features the Bulleid-Firth-Brown style of wheels were incorporated into his unique 500hp 0-6-0 diesel shunting and local freight locomotive design. Devised before Nationalisation it was not completed at Ashford Works until 1950. While credited with a top speed of 43mph it was perhaps a serious midway diesel-mechanical alternative to what would become the standard shunting locomotive rated at 350hp. It was based initially at Norwood Junction, then briefly at Feltham before heading to Leeds for around ten months. It was then laid up at Derby Works for almost two years before being sent to work at Hornsey for just over three months. Finally, it returned to Norwood Junction who sometimes sent it out on local goods workings until it required more serious repairs. This is when it was sent home to Ashford Works where it remained dumped for most of 1959 until it was scrapped by the end of the year. *Rail Photoprints*

Opposite: Even before the Leader debacle the Southern Railway had decided to build three 1Co-Co1 diesel-electric locomotives, to which Bulleid once again applied some of his ideas upon style, including the wheels! Being sent out on such prestige working means that the operating department must have faith in the locomotive, as 10201 brings the down Bournemouth Belle through Vauxhall in 1953. *Rail Photoprints*

Before stepping aside Bulleid managed to inject his influence into the batch of thirty-six 350hp 0-6-0 diesel shunters being constructed for the Southern Region at Ashford Works. Although to the then more or less standard design except these would have his Bullied-Firth-Brown wheelsets rather than the traditional spoked variety used elsewhere. The first of the class 15211, is seen brand new in black complete without any British Railways markings as yet but with neatly painted front numbers at Ashford in April 1949, she would be allocated to Norwood Junction for her entire working life until withdrawn in December 1971. Likewise, 15214 followed on a month later from here at Ashford Works where she was pictured ready for traffic on 7 May 1949.
Photos: Strathwood Library Collection & Colour Rail

Opposite: Also entrusted to the Bournemouth Belle once again during 1953 was 10202 seen departing Southampton Central albeit in less than pristine condition for such a working. The first two locomotives were rated at 1,750hp and weighed in at a massive 135tons upon completion at Brighton Works during 1950/51. The first locomotive 10201 spent nine months of 1951 on show at the Festival of Britain Exhibition, rather than working. *Colour Rail*

The final locomotive of the trio 10203 was to enter service after a gap of a few years rated at 2,000hp with a slightly reduced weight of 132tons in March 1954. This was perhaps its first official service train judging from the officials in hats busying themselves before departure from Waterloo on 17 June 1954. We can easily see the locomotive was designed to match the profile of Bulleid's coaching stock. *Rail Online*

Approval was given for two Co-Co electric mixed traffic locomotives to be built at Ashford Works for the Central Section with the first as CC1 arriving in 1941. Now renumbered as 20001 we see her setting off from Chichester with a lengthy goods for Norwood Junction in the early 1950s. *Rail Archive Stephenson*

Although the design of the first two looked to be pure Bulleid from the matching cab style to his EMU stock and his Bulleid-Firth-Brown wheels incorporated into the bogie frames, it was the Southern Railway's Chief Electrical Engineer Alfred Raworth who influenced the electrical side of things. Fresh from a recent overhaul 20002 is pushed out of Brighton's Works on 20 June 1951 by their resident Terrier 377S. Capable of working not only from the third rail, the Southern also equipped several yards with overhead wiring, hence the pantographs. A sensible safety wise yet expensive solution that was seldom used to prevent electrocution of staff within shunting yards. *The Bluebell Museum Archive*

The final Bulleid/Raworth electric locomotive 20003 to be built at Ashford Works emerged after Nationalisation in September 1948 for trials at Brighton, where we see it being inspected within the confines of the steam shed's yard. With its gleaming malachite green paint and Bulleid favoured lining suggesting how the great man perhaps saw the future. Although he left British Railways a year later, his influence was then to be felt across the Irish Sea with further radical design ideas beyond the scope of this book. *Rail Archive Stephenson*